Storytelling Secrets

Secrets of being an Amazing Public Speaker and Conversationalist

Table of Contents

About the Author 3
Introduction 4
Chapter One: Storytelling 5
Chapter Two: Having an Attractive Personality 8
Chapter Three: Get Excited 11
Chapter Four: Getting Over Your Fear of Speaking in Public 16
Chapter Five: Work with Your Body 24
Chapter Six: Connecting with Your Audience 31
Chapter Seven: The Power of Your Voice 38
Chapter Eight: Tips to Dazzle Your Audience 44
Chapter Ten: The Psychology Behind Storytelling 54
Conclusion 58

About the Author

Bradley Heaton is an endeavored 40 year old man who does a lot of speaking within his company of which he is the go-to man to making in-house announcements and speeches. Bradley enjoys the fact that his word is heard out a lot but also the fact that he can listen a lot. His main role in his company is recruitment where he hires many candidates to his company everyday where needed but is also the top of his class for human resource management. Being an executive of a small-medium company he understands that management and organization is the key to success and deserves to be treated with all due respect.

In his spare time, Bradley enjoys driving cars of which his favorite brand is Porsche and owns classics and modern day Porsches. A die hard Porsche fan, he hates to see his brand being defeated by the competition just like how he hates being defeated in business and will strive to be the best possible in his field.

F1 is his favorite sport because of the technicalities of it all. His favorite team on F1 is McLaren with his current favorite driver of the time this is being written being Sebastian Vettel even though he doesn't race for McLaren.

In his other spare time he spends time with his family of which he has two children and a lovely wife. One child is named Emily and the other is named James. He hopes that they will both become speakers and will be just as great as he is in his career and if not better than him.

Introduction

Not every person was born a storyteller, some of us have to take classes, read books, and follow lessons in order to transform into a great storyteller.

I was one of those people that had to gain knowledge to become the storyteller I am today - I didn't want to settle for just being a storyteller, I wanted to be amazing. You know, the type of storyteller that captures attention from the very beginning to end, the type that sticks in people's minds when they leave the building at the end of the show... that's who I wanted to be and that is who I am today.

Wouldn't you like to be a great storyteller? Of course you would, or you wouldn't be reading this right now. Like I said before, I wasn't born this way, it took a large amount of trial and error to get to where I am today – now, I am able to capture my audience right away... how? That is what I am going to tell you...

Chapter One: Storytelling

The ability to tell a story… now that right there is one of the most powerful skills anyone can have. We're not talking about just any story, we're talking about the ability to take a normal story and turn it into something that becomes enticing, captivating, and leaves the listener either feeling on top of the world, or bursting with laughter … or maybe leaving them in aw, on the verge of tears.

The listener could be your neighbor, someone you met at the local café, or an auditorium packed with listeners that are waiting to be inspired … it could be a group of children, or maybe even your own children as you're tucking them into bed for a good night's sleep.

While being a natural storyteller is great, because this means they already possess those skills needed to tell a good story. However, the good news here is that anyone, yes, even you, can learn how to become a natural storyteller. All you need is the proper tools and strategies (which we're giving you now), and the willingness to get into action and improve the skill of storytelling.

Stories can be used in every setting throughout the world. They are the way to spread new ideas, and the backbone of new relationships.

What is Storytelling and Why is it Important?

In this section, we're going to give you a brief background on storytelling and tell you how it is used before we jump into the methods of how to make a story inspiring, powerful, and unforgettable.

The art of storytelling is something that has been around since the beginning of time. You can define it as an ancient art form that gives people the opportunity to actively express their thoughts and ideas in an interactive way that stimulates the imagination of the listener.

Storytelling is a two way street. You have the storyteller, then you have your listener. The way the listener responds to the storyteller normally dictates the teller's next move, depending on what type of response they are looking for.

Let's take a good comedian, as an example. Comedians listen to the response of the audience in order to determine the direction he should take next. Is he seeking more laughter? Does he want them to be shocked? Does he want an emotional response? Does he want them to be shocked? Whatever type of response he is looking for, he has the ability to get it by reading and listening to the impact of his story on the audience in front of him.

Storytellers use both body language and spoken language in order to express the events and characters in the story often through vocalization and physical movement.

The Social Experience

Storytelling has always been a good form of entertainment. It can provide a fun experience for both adults and children. People can be so caught up in a story that, before you know it, the person is laughing hysterically, or they may get an annoyed expression in their eyes, depending on the type of story you're telling. Stories have the capacity of eliciting emotional responses and are great ways to immediately connect with another individual.

Chapter Two: Having an Attractive Personality

Oh yes, an attractive personality is a must. People who have dull personalities... I'm sorry, you're not going to get very far with that personality. When you speak, you need to speak in an attractive manner and put emphases on your words. If you sit there and read as if you are reading from a script, people are going to lose interest, get up out of their seats and walk away, never to return again.

Let me ask you a question – what is the thing that makes people come flocking to them? What is the secret to that magnetic personality they have? Charisma and a ridiculous amount of it... Anyone who is wishing to be a better storyteller will take the time to learn this art and master it. Mastering anything including having an amazing charisma takes 10,000 hours according to experts so you better start soon!

A Great Drive to Succeed:

Those individuals that have deep determination have a tendency to value their time too much to waste it on efforts that are meaningless. People have a tendency to fall for those that have a sense of purpose and direction... those that are determined are those that are more likely to make a difference.

Communicate Considerately:

Speak sincerely. Listen lovingly. Be present in the moment with others by showing that you care.

Look for the Best in Others:

You need to be looking for the best for others because if you don't then you won't look genuine. You could do the "fake it till you make it" but it's really hard to fake something without others seeing through you. And do you really want to be fake? If you're fake, you lose your reputation and that's your life gone if you can't control it. Looking for the best for others is very important.

Enthusiasm:

Enthusiasm is probably the most important thing because it's the most outward part of our personality excluding being an extrovert and introvert. Enthusiasm shows passion in yourself and if you're directing that enthusiasm at others then you're showing passion in them too. Enthusiasm is super important, you can't be that boring guy at the back of the room.

Humor is a Good Thing:

If you want to take the funny approach to storytelling then having humor is obviously a key thing. If you plan on being a funny storyteller then you may as well not be a speaker. Humor relieves stress because it changes from the stressy topic to the new topic which has an amazing start already. It's really at engaging others because you are making others laugh.

Calm and Composed:

You may have noticed that those with attractive personalities are normally calm and composed. With this comes a health self-esteem level. Besides, having this type of attitude will put others at ease right away.

Just Smile:

Whenever people judge a person's personality without knowing them is how much they smile. Smiling shows how much you actually care about other things around you. It shows your inner heart and personality. You are the type of person who is easily approachable which a huge plus for anybody. It also has an engagement part to it because smiles are contagious.

Don't Worry:

So many people lack in the storytelling niche because they are too worried about what others are thinking of them. Stop worrying about what others are thinking of you and just live and be yourself. Let them think what they want to think about towards you, don't worry about making a good impression. Like I said before, just be yourself. By showing your true colors, others will love your honesty.

Adopting these key points isn't a walk in the park because they will take years and years of experience to perfect them but starting early is always a good thing. The best thing is that we can all do these so do them now!

Chapter Three: Get Excited

A good storyteller will be taking their audience on an amazing journey, leaving them feeling motivated and inspired. Yes, structuring your speech in a manner that will help you get your ideas across to your audience, while keeping their attention, can be a bit tricky as well.

When you start off, what do you do? Do you start with the facts you would like to get across? That's the wrong route to take. Human minds are hardwired for stories - they love journeys, heroes, layers, surprises, and of course, happy endings.

Standing up in front of a room full of people, even if the room will only have three people or less, can cause anxiety and fear. As you are getting ready for the presentation, you may have a myriad of questions running through your mind, including whether people will like what you have to present, if your voice will shake, whether you are adequately prepared – the list of questions is endless. When you're anxious, your thought process turns towards the negative, and as your presentation gets closer, you end up feeling worse than ever. These fears can lead to things going wrong for you during your presentation, which would lead you to believe these things were destined to go around.

Do you want to know my very own secret to giving an electrifying presentation? It involves getting excited about it! Take a basketball player, as an example – he's getting ready to represent his country for the first time on the global arena. He has put in a large amount of work when training, he has gone through all the drills and he is fully prepared to face any outcome that may occur. When going into the game, he doesn't have fear that things will take a turn for the worse. All he has is enthusiasm and excitement flowing through his veins as he anticipates being able to reveal his best moves and please the audience that is watching him.

Before you start your presentation, have some positive affirmations repeating through your mind. These could include "the audience will love me" or "this is going to be fun." By turning to positive affirmations, you can rest with the satisfaction of knowing that this will put you in the right frame of mind, and you will be confident enough to stand up in front of an audience, regardless of how big or small they may be.

Here's some tips that will help you get excited for your next storytelling event...

Be Prepared – If you really want to get excited about storytelling, you need to be prepared. This will involve taking the required time to practice your performance until you are sure it is perfect. You should go through a rehearsal every night, or every other night – this will give you a peace of mind when you're standing in front of that audience. When you are preparing, tell the story out loud so that you can hear yourself and see what you sound like. When you're rehearsing, pay attention to your tone. Do this on your own, then once you're ready, have a friend or family member listen to you. If you want to know what you look like when you're telling the story, you can use a video camera.

Be Creative – As you are getting prepared to tell that story, your primary goal is to engage your readers. A technique you should focus on is the way that you will be telling your story – there are several methods that you can choose from, depending on the result you prefer to achieve. You can choose from these techniques: Spark Lines and The Mountain... I will be discussing both of these techniques towards the end of this chapter.

End the Story on a High Note – The ending to your story should be powerful and strong. It should be so powerful that it is able to call your audience to action. This will require you to emphasize some of the key points that you mentioned when you first started out, which will help show how your presentation has gone full circle. When the audience leaves, they need to leave with the mindset that they can make the next move.

When it comes to getting excited, you will need to learn how to think outside of that box while telling your story. You will need to develop various ways to use visual aids, and you may even want to consider how you can dress to add life to your story. When it comes to your presentation, have a goal in mind – this goal is based on what you want you want from your audience as your end game

Let's look at the different storytelling structures that I told you about earlier…

The Mountain:

This is a structure that is used to map the tension and drama when telling a story. The Mountain doesn't necessarily have an ending that is happy. In the first part, you'll be setting the scene, which will be followed by a series of small challenges, and a rise to action before the climactic conclusion.

Think of this structure as a TV series. Each episode will have its own ups and downs, all building to the finale that takes place at the end of the season.

The Mountain is Good For:

- Slowly building tension with the audience
- Showing your audience how to overcome obstacles in a series of challenges
- Delivering a conclusion that is satisfying

Sparklines:

This is a way to map presentation structures. The best of speeches success because they take our ordinary world and contract it with an ideal, improved world. Basically, it compares what is with what could be. Does that make sense?

Sparklines creates a desire for change within the audience. This is an emotional technique that will motivate your audience to follow you.

Sparklines are Good For:

- Creating excitement
- Inspiring the audience

Petal Structure:

This is a structure that you would use if you were to organize multiple stories or speakers around one main concept. If you have various unconnected stories you would like to tell, or even things you would like to reveal, this is the structure you would be using.

This involves telling your stories one by one, before you turn back to the main story. You can overlap the petals as one story introduces to the next, but each story within itself should be a complete narrative.

This form of storytelling will show your audience how these key stories are related to each other. This will leave them feeling the true importance of your story.

The Petal is Good for:

- Showing how various scenarios relate to one main idea.
- Demonstrating how strands of the story are connected.

You see, storytelling, within itself, is an art – this is something you can make or break, depending on the "picture" you choose to paint. You can make it exciting and really captivate your audience, or you can make it boring and chase your audience straight out the door. The path you take is fully up to you – which one of these storytelling methods will you use?

Chapter Four: Getting Over Your Fear of Speaking in Public

Let's start out by giving your fear a name – some people refer to it as "stage fright," while others go for the more technical term "glossophobia."

Glossophobia is also known as speech anxiety. It comes from the Greek word glossa (tongue) and phobos (dread or fear). This is a severe fear of public speaking, or speaking in general. It is one of the most common phobias in the world today. About 75 percent of the world is suffering from it, but in different degrees. This is something that is experienced by more people than claustrophobia (the fear of being enclosed) or even agoraphobia (the fear of heights,) and arachnophobia (the fear of spiders).

Some symptoms of glossophonbia include the following:

- Freezing up in front of your audience
- Dry mouth
- Nausea
- Dizziness
- Numbing of the hands
- Shortness of breath
- Shaking
- Panic attacks
- Sweating
- Shaky Voice

Professionals have even stated that the dread felt by some students about being called on by the teacher to stand up in front of the class or to answer a question is an early manifestation of glossophobia.

So, what causes the fear of speaking in public? There are numerous reasons that can be blamed as the cause of one's fear of speaking in public...

One's Upbringing or Environment While Growing Up – Those individuals that grew up in an environment that does not help build up their courage and confidence to deal with crowds, or even having conversations with many people tend to lack confidence and have low self-esteem levels. As a result, this will shun the idea of having to speak in public.

Traumatic Experiences – There are times where the individual may have had an actual past experience of speaking in public and ended up having an extremely embarrassing moment. Kinds that had this type of experience have a tendency to shy away from having to be exposed to such situations ever again, because they fear the embarrassing moment could be repeated.

Lack of Familiarity with the Concept of Speaking in Public – Individuals have a tendency to be afraid of what they're not familiar with. So, naturally, those individuals that haven't been exposed to public speaking are going to naturally feel nervous when it is their time to stand up in the spotlight

Speech Problems – There are individuals that have speech problems such as stuttering. Those individuals have a tendency to be wary of speaking in public.

Treatment to Help Get Over the Fear of Public Speaking:

Therapy – A cognitive-behavioral therapy is a common treatment that is suggested for those individuals who would like to get rid of their fear of public speaking. Through cognitive-behavioral therapy, these individuals will have the opportunity to learn how to replace the messages of fear that they receive with more positive thoughts and self-talk. This form of therapy is especially effective for those individuals who experience panic attacks when they're faced with the idea of standing up and speaking in public. Through this treatment option, the individual will learn effective relaxation techniques that they can use to handle such attacks. Once they are able to get a handle on these attacks, they will be easier to control.

Virtual Reality Therapy – Some swear that virtual reality therapy is also effective to help those individuals that are dealing with social anxiety. Basically, through this type of therapy, the individual will be placed in a virtual environment that simulates speaking in public. Here, they will be asked to deliver their speeches again and again, as if they are experiencing the real thing.

Medications – Yes, there are actual medications that individuals can have subscribed to them. These medications can help control the patient's fears or nerves. However, more often than not, these medications are meant to be taken while the patient is undergoing cognitive-behavioral therapy, and not taken on their own. There are various beta blocked people use in order to find relief from extreme terror or nerves. The beta-blocking drugs help ease performance anxiety because they have properties in them that are capable of blocking the action of adrenaline. Users should be wary, though, because there are certain side effects that can occur while using such medications. This is the reason why this form of treatment is approached with caution.

Self-Help – This is an option that normally pops up after the patient has handled their fear. These methods are focused on ensuring that the control that the patient has over their fear of speaking in public is permanent. In other words, medications and therapy will help the individual get past their fear of public speaking, while self-help techniques will aid in their confidently presenting in front of an audience or a crowd.

Choosing the Best Treatment Option:

While there are a large variety of treatment options available for people to use, not all of them work for every single person. Therefore, when you're choosing which treatment option you should follow, it is important that you consider the following:

The Cause of the Fear – What's causing the fear to begin with? Is it because of a traumatic event that took place in the past that is hard to get over? Is it due to a stuttering problem? Or are you just too shy to even contemplate speaking in front of people?

In order for you to know what to address, you must first know what the root cause of your irrational fear of speaking in public is.

The True Nature of the Fear – What are you afraid of? Could it be the fact that you may mistake fear of performance as a whole with fear of speaking in public? There are individuals that are comfortable with speaking in front of a group of people, but then, when they have to perform something else, they freeze up. For example, some actors are comfortable when they're speaking lines on a stage, but when they're being interviewed, they shut down.

Learning what you're really afraid of will make it easier to determine the type of treatment you need to take in order to fix your fear of speaking in public.

The Severity of the Problem – This one pertains to the intensity of the fear. It could be solved by attending various consoling sessions. On another note, there are also causes where both medications and cognitive-behavioral therapy is needed.

Here's a little fact for you – Do you know the professional golfer, Tiger Woods? He grew up with a speech impediment. Unbelievable, right? Sure, when you look at him today, you won't be able to tell, but he grew up stuttering, which made him afraid of public speaking. When asked how he got past this, he said that he focused on fixing his speech impediment. He continued practicing, and having nice conversation with his dog, and always kept a positive attitude on things. He continuously pictured himself in a positive place in order to keep his mind on the right path. Thinking about it, I bet you could learn a lot from how he conquered his own fear. To start with, he identified the cause of the problem and concentrated on fixing it before he moved forward. When he discovered the root of the problem, he was persistent and never gave up until he got the results he longed for.

Take Your Time – I understand, you want to start speaking in public right away … or maybe you don't, maybe you're too afraid to right now, but you want to get over this fear so that you can look forward to storytelling. It is important that you don't rush things.

Don't Rush Through the Story – On the same note, it is important that you don't rush through the story. Yes, you will be in a hurry to get it done and over with as quickly as possible, so you may feel the urge to rush through the story. However, fast talking has a tendency to make it difficult to breath.

Research has suggested three key things you should do when you find yourself experiencing fear of standing in front of people and telling a story:

Don't Show Your Fear – To do this, keep your face blank (or relaxed). Also, control any trembling you may experience in your hands and limbs.

Stand Still – If you're restless, especially when you're on stage, this is a sign that you're anxious.

Don't Speak too Fast – If you speak too fast, you'll probably end up stuttering, which is only going to worsen the problem. Choose your words carefully and enunciate them. What if you talk too slow? At least then, the people around you will be able to comprehend you.

Further Tips on Getting Over the Fear of Speaking in Public:

Take Training Courses – There are classes and courses you can attend. These classes are related directly to public speaking and can be beneficial if you're looking to get over glossophobia. These classes will help you overcome this fear, but they will also teach you how to be more confident while speaking in public.

Join Support Groups Be More Proactive – Have you joined support groups? That's a good step, but you shouldn't stop there. Expand that social network by taking initiative in joining more groups and participating in activities that will expose you to more people. Drama class, for example, would be a great step. Before you know it, you'll be more at ease with the idea of communicating with more than three people at a time.

Join Organizations – There's various organizations you can join that will reinforce what you have learned so far. If will get you started in practicing speaking in small groups, until you're able to work your way up to a larger audience.

Give Your Mind a Workout – Take at least five minutes a day to yourself and try to medicate, allowing your mind to have a good workout. Sit down in a quiet place with your spine straight and supported by the back of a comfortable chair. Close your eyes and just breathe. Regulate your breathing so that you can feel the air go in and out. When your mind begins to wander, focus on your breathing. This will bring you back to your focus point.

Practice Makes Perfect – That's right, practice makes perfect! Just like Tiger Woods did, you need to practice and don't give up.

No matter how hard you think it is right now, eventually, it's going to get easy. Start out by telling stories that you personally love and have knowledge on.

Chapter Five: Work with Your Body

By properly using your body to tell stories, it will be as if your soul is telling the story, making it more attention grabbing. Put it this way – which would you rather listen to, someone who blandly stands there, without moving any limbs and tells a story, or someone who uses their body to tell the story? Personally, I get bored when someone stands there and tells a story, without having any emotion whatsoever… it just doesn't flow well.

Both your voice and your body are powerful tools you can use in order to enhance communication… fortunately, both of these are easy to train. They can be conditioned, just like a muscle in order to support storytelling. In this chapter of the book, I am going to tell you how to work with your

Using Gestures in Public Speaking:

Let's start out by talking about gestures. Gestures, with a simple rule, can support your meaning. It is important that you do not use gestures that detract from what you're talking about, because those are bad.

Make sure you plan your gestures before you are telling your story. Creature the conditions for the gesture, instead of the gesture within itself. Before you know it, at the appropriate moment, the right gesture will come about. The audience will see something that is natural and will more than likely be supportive of what you're saying.

Don't forget to breathe, then breath again, then again… it is important that you recognize the most important thing is to make sure you are comfortable – this will make it easier for you to tell your story. If you're working from a secure place, you will be able to access your intellect, preparation, and imagination easier when you have even breathing.

Start out from the neutral position. This means you should have your hands at your side, bringing your hands up to make the gesture. When you make the gesture, make sure it's definitive and clean. Don't ever make a repetitive gesture, or a halfway one. After you make your gesture, naturally return your hands to the "neutral" position.

What does gesturing accomplish? Honestly, gesturing can help you accomplish a variety of things. Gestures help support what you're saying, and it tells the audience that you are confident, because you're not placing your hands between each other.

Descriptive Gestures:

Descriptive gestures are gestures that you can use to describe something or a story. It carries a lot weight when others are looking at you because it shows passion. No one likes someone who is just standing there with their arms by their side.

Obviously the most obvious form of descriptive gestures is using your hands. You can do so just doing some random hand waving gestures showing interaction to the audience or you can actually use them descriptively. Such as whenever you are describing something big, you can literally just open your arms really wide. Whilst we're on this example, it can also show contrasts such you showing something really small then something really big. This will show what you're describing and will engage others.

You can also use them to show quantity, numbers, objects and so on. These gestures are extremely useful when you're telling a story, you can't really tell a good story with only using your words. By using descriptive gestures, we can create a deeper feeling of our story and improve the retention of our listeners.

Emotional Gestures:

Don't forget about emphatic gestures, also referred to as emotional gestures. For example, when you're sad, you play yourself down (physically) and tell the sad part of the story. When you're at an angry part of the story, you may pretend to punch the air around you and put that angry face on. Basically, you need to use those gestures to symbolize the feelings you have during the story. Emphatic gestures will help you appear more genuine as you're telling the story.

Don't Force it – Simply put it, when you force something, it looks very fake unless you're a professional faker. Being fake isn't good for anything as said before and all you'll do is hurt yourself in the long run. It really all comes to good preparation and practice before actually telling your story. Let the gestures out themselves, don't let your brain control your arms, let your mouth control them.

Try to stay away from gestures that don't add any value or are irrelevant to your story. This can hurt your presentation by sending two different messages which can either show that you don't know what you're talking about or that you're forcing it out. Just let everything out naturally.

Examples of bad gestures that I see are playing with your hair, this is a terrible one for ladies because it's just there waiting to be played. Adjusting clothes is another terrible gesture. It may be an essential gesture most of the time but avoid it the majority of the time because it can show little preparation.

Your Physical Expression:

When you're telling that story in public, don't forget about the art of physical expression. The expression you have on your face during the story can make or break the entire ordeal. If you're at a happy part of the story, have a happy expression, if you're at a sad part of the story, obviously you shouldn't still have that happy expression on your face. Make sure your expressions change as you tell the story. So, take the interesting things you have to tell your audience, and find the physical expression that matches the story.

The Power of the Pause:

When you're telling that story, especially if you're new to storytelling, pausing is the hardest thing you can try the first time. In everyday conversation, people have a surplus of pause simply because they don't know what they want to talk about. But since you're more prepared in a speech its harder to create a pause with your excitement trying to burst out.

In human psychology, we feel like we have to provide value in every single moment and in the case of a speech, its word. We feel like we have to make our essays as long as possible even though it's usually not the length by the quality of it.

We will also increase the anticipation of what's coming up because what's the point in making such a big deal if it's not significant? Anticipation creates retention which is what you want from a story.

Let me tell you how to use the power of the pause...

Start out with silence. I understand, it takes some huge balls at times to stand up in front of an audience which you've never met before after you have been introduced on stage and not say anything right away, but this is the most impactful way of creating the attention you require. It creates a questioning environment with people paying attention because they want to know the answer. It also creates tension due to the skepticism our brain automatically makes.

When it's your turn to tell the story, start out by standing their quietly as you gaze over the people in the audience, letting them make eye contact back with you. Once you feel everyone is comfortable and waiting for your story with anticipation, start with a dynamic story.

Trust me, you're going to be astonished by the amount of attention this brings out. Since you have created a bond through silence, the audience will be ready for you to make your big announcement, just make sure you don't screw up on this because it's bad if you screw up.

Pause with Purpose:

During parts of the story, there are times where the pause can add importance and give the audience a chance to laugh, absorb or adjust to what you just said. When you have just told the points in a story, just stop talking for five seconds. It allows us to absorb your points and also to take notes of it. Yes, we need a break from what people are saying absorb it and take note of it. If someone says they don't then they're lying.

Transition with Pauses:

When you're telling that story, if you're jumping from one part of the story to the other, without warning, you'll be leaving your listeners behind with confused looks on their faces. This is because you didn't pause and give them time to catch up with the story you're telling. When this type of stuff happens, listeners have a tendency to stop listening to what you're saying even if they may look like they're looking at you. On another note, when you time pause correctly you're giving the listeners a chance to prepare for the next part of your story.

Twitching:

Most people have a nervous twitch that becomes more noticeable when they're doing an activity that can cause them additional anxiety. These nervous movements will affect the quality of the presentation and include tapping of the feet, shifting your weight from one to the other, or swaying without cause. To find out what is going on when you tell your story, you should record yourself and watch the playback. This way, you will see which part of the presentation you need to work on to improve.

Drink Water:

At least ten minutes before it's time to go up in front of your audience, you should have a glass of water. This is because when you're anxious in any way, you're likely to end up with a dry mouth. The clarity of your voice may be affected as you don't have enough saliva to swallow. The water will help prevent your tongue from sticking to the roof of your mouth as you're telling that story.

Move with Style:

Have you ever watched presenters? There are those that love to move up and down the stage, so much that your eyes and neck may get exhausted from trying to keep up with them. Then, you have those who are so rigid, that even their voiced come out with a monotone. If you're looking to tell your story in a nice persuasive manner, you need to incorporate some movement into it. Allow yourself to slowly walk on stage, stopping your movement when you want to emphasize a point. Mind you, this is nothing like erratic pacing up and down the stage, which is merely a sign of being nervous. From time to time, move towards the audience, because this will capture their attention more.

In the end, as you're telling that story, make so you do so with style. As you move around on the stage, move around gracefully and with style – be the charismatic self you were born to be and you shouldn't have a problem winning your audience over.

Chapter Six: Connecting with Your Audience

The worst case scenario that anyone can find themselves when up on that stage is when you've forgotten what you were going to say. You trip, mix and stumble over your own words. You end up rambling about something that you can't backtrack from which usually ends up being something completely irrelevant to your actual speech. You will start to sweat and panic at this point, your speech falls to pieces. Probably the nightmare we all have when speaking in front of an audience.

We've all been here struggling to catch a grip of ourselves and it's pretty painful and embarrassing. Getting up in front of people and telling a story, regardless of the story it may be, is not easy at all. You have to make sure that you're not wasting your audience's time as well as your own. Then you have another commitment to make sure that they listen such as making your story relating to them.

In this chapter I'll teach you how to connect and relate to your audience because the last thing you want is to fail them.

In its purest form a story is just some talking. Talking is obviously something we all know about since we do It no matter what. Talking is literally just exchanging information from one mouth to another ones ear and vice versa. It's seems a lot easier when you put it like that but on stage, it's obviously much harder than that.

You're just as the storyteller is to make a connection with the people in front of you so that they will openly listen to you. If you don't get your audience's attention, you're going to lose their interest within seconds, and the story you're telling will be a waste of time. Surely, you don't want that, do you?

Let me introduce you to some amazing ways to connect with your audience as you're telling that story...

Make Sure you Have the Right Audience:

This right here may seem basic, but how do you know what your audience likes? You can't be talking sport to a bunch of business people or by the end of the speech, they'll be no one left to listen to you.

The majority of use tell a story because we have a nice topic to talk about that in our heads may be interesting. Most of the time the audience doesn't have any contribution to this story other than turning up. Whenever you are doing a speech, you have to make sure that you know what audience you're targeting, it sounds simple. Simple but simple is always obvious. Too many people think that their speech is going to be the thing that changes everyone's lives no matter what background they have. It's like the one friend who think they have the billion dollar app idea that will change everyone but it simply doesn't.

You need to do some basics such as whenever setting up your event, make sure you're labelling correctly and not some sentence or word. Get your audience to contribute a little such as creating a survey using Survey Monkey and ask them what they want to hear. There's no point in speaking to people who aren't interested.

Preparation is key so asking beforehand is always going to make you win rather than improvising whilst on stage only to stumble over your own words. Just contact or ask some of your audience to what they want because it'll make your speech far better.

Have a Good Sense of Humor:

A good sense of humor will normally pay off. A common theme that I've seen is that a lot of speeches including mine start off with a joke. A pause then a joke. When the speech start off with a joke, you basically give the permission to release all tension and just chill.

A pause will make them pay attention like they're in trouble then a joke will relieve it all which will create retention in their brain. Spreading jokes like its butter all over your story will keep your audience engaged and something to looking forward to (if your jokes are good).

Be Yourself:

This piece of advice is repeated everywhere today almost to the point of being trite, but it is no less true for that. The person you are is the one who experienced and created the story, so your telling will be a lot more authentic if you allow your character to shine through.

Talk About your Most Vulnerable Positions of Life:

Do you really want to make a connection with your audience? Of course you do!

Nothing beats a story that rarely anyone tells anyone else, a story that shows the struggle you had or even how others have treated you. Don't sugarcoat any of it not even the worst bits, you show the loose, broken and sobbing moments.

The audience that you're speaking is to will have the most utter respect for you because they'll know you're genuine and not some fake selling them something useless. Remember that being genuine is the best way of engaging an audience because we can all see through someone else bullshitting us very easily.

You may put yourself in an uncomfortable position and probably embarrassing such has having to maybe sell yourself to make ends meet. But as with everything in life, nothings easy. You have to show everyone your true colors with no hue change.

Give Back to your Audience:

When I say give back something to your audience, I mean give them real value. Value such as leads for their business, a guide or a service. You should not only give them something of value but also a piece of physical memorabilia. If you give them something like a metal ornament which is esthetically pleasing to the eye then your audience may put on their table then it will remind them of you.

Just give them a service/useful product and a piece of memorabilia and you'll have them back to your next speech in no time.

Eye Contact:

Don't forget just how important it is to make eye contact. Mind you, don't stare at one audience member the entire time, alternate between the audience members. Eye contact is one of the best ways to connect with your audience.

Passion:

The only way your audience is going to connect with you is if you are passionate about the story you are telling. You need to love the topic that you are talking about and having your information at your fingertips will give the audience the confidence that they can trust what you have to say, and that they can view you as an expert in your own right.

Slide Succession:

Have you ever heard of this one? It's a secret to connecting with your audience. It involves being aware of everything that is within your presentation. You should be able to seamlessly move from one slide to another, and place your focus on the audience rather than looking back at the information that is one the slide. When you are not organized or aware of the order of your slides in the presentation, you are able to foster confusion in your audience, as you try to recover from an unexpected slide.

Silence:

In all your speaking, you should never underestimate the power of silence. Its first use should be just after you stand up to speak or enter the stage. After any applause and cheering have died down, pause for a moment before launching into your story. You'll notice that this is something every professional public speaker does, from presidents and politicians to standup comedians, television hosts and more. This moment of silence has benefits for you and your audience: it gives you an opportunity to collect your thoughts, take a deep breath and begin your story strongly, and it allows the audience to settle down and be prepared to absorb your message.

Your posture:

Avoid slouching. Everything about you on stage should exude confidence.

Your facial expressions:

It's really important to pay attention to these as they are the most prominent non-verbal way to communicate your feelings. As a general rule, you should wear a friendly, sociable smile when you are telling your story. If the subject of your story swings wide on either side on the scale of emotion, then you can adopt a base facial expression more in keeping with it – grave for a more somber story and more excited for a lighter, funnier story. Your story will have upswings and downswings of emotion, though – alter your expressions to go with them.

Focus your Attention:

When giving a presentation, your nervousness may have you focusing on yourself too much, worrying about what you are wearing, how you are standing, whether you have a hair out of place, and what is happening with your body movements. To connect with your audience, you cannot appear to be highly self-conscious and confused. You need to show your audience that you understand them. Giving them a blank stare can make certain members of your audience uncomfortable, as can simple looking at one section of your audience as you give your presentation. The other people may feel unimportant. What you need to do is focus your attention on something that is outside yourself, which will help you better connect with the audience. Consider focusing on something like spectacles. While giving your presentation, look from one person to the other to see how many people are wearing spectacles. This will keep your eyes moving in a subtle way, and will prevent uncomfortable stares or strange silences. From spectacles, you can choose to focus on people wearing the color black, and after than you can focus on something else.

Try to be Funny:

Electrifying presentations have elements within them that are lighthearted and put the audience in a good mood. This is done by being funny where appropriate, and adding humor to the presentation. You can use humor to emphasize a serious point, by getting the audience to laugh and then going into the graveness of a situation. Humor is also excellent at the start of the presentation to break the ice and get them to connect with you. At the end of the presentation, humor will lead the audience to remember how you are finishing up, and any points that you make to finalize.

Finally, as you are telling your story, you need to learn to have faith in your ideas and abilities, and be as original as possible. You can draw some information from others, including execution techniques, but your information should be your own, your delivery should represent you well, and the entire presentation should have the stamp of your personality with it. This will connect with your audience, and lead them to remember you in all situations.

Excellent presentations are those that inspire an audience, and the tools that you use for the presentation should have everything necessary to support and questions that may arise at the conclusion of the presentations to prompt intellectual discussions. Ensure that you have slick and flexible transitions and as much as possible, use motion to keep the members of the audience attentive.

Chapter Seven: The Power of Your Voice

You may not realize it right now, but regardless of how you sound, your voice is powerful ... it may not be powerful every time you talk, but when you put forth a certain tone and emphasis, it can sound powerful. One of the biggest secrets behind a successful presentation involves modulating the tone of your voice. In this chapter, I am going to introduce you to the power of your voice, so pay close attention to what I have to tell you...

Topic and Tone:

Let's start out with the topic and tone of your voice. The topic and tone should directly reflect what your presentation topic is about.

For example, if you are anting to convince your audience to take an action after your story is over, then the tone of your voice should be gentle and imploring towards them. By using the tone of your voice and the story, you should be able to call your audience into a deep thought so that they can make a good decision. If you would like people to make a revolutionary charge, your tone should instead be powerful, and the words that flow from your mouth should inspire your audience to get up right away and do something to make a change.

When you're giving good news, if you use a tone that is monotonic, this will take away from the excitement that you're trying to portray.

With grave news, it is important that you do not come off as exciting. Changing the tone of your voice so that it fits the meaning of your topic can move your audience in the direction you're seeking, or, if you do it wrong, it could have the opposite effect on your audience and upset them.

During your rehearsal, try working with the tone of your voice and try different tones to see which one sounds better. You need to find one that gives a strong message. Listen to yourself out loud, or have a friend listen so that they can give you feedback. This will protect yourself from undermining the message you are trying to bring forth to your audience.

Pronunciation and Accent:

Have you ever sat down and watched a documentary in English that is speaking to different people from all over the world? They are all speaking the same language, and in some cases you may notice the words are written at the bottom of the screen so that you can read them and understand what is said. This is because it is believed that for some, it is difficult to make out the words that were said because of the accent.

Make sure people are able to understand you. When you're telling that story, you need to realize that you have an accent whenever any person is listening to you. This is going to affect your speech, pronunciation and clarity. You're not expected to alter the way you speak every single time you tell a story so that people can understand you, but you do need to learn how to speak more clearly. This is going to require you to speak slowly, especially if you are starting your story.

This will help your audience familiarize yourself with the accent you may have. After a couple of minutes, your audience will be adjusted to the way you are speaking, so you should be able to pick up the pace.

The Way You Speak to Your Audience:

The way you speak to your audience is another secret to an excellent presentation. Don't speak as if you're speaking at them, speak as if you're speaking with them.

When your presentation feels like you're giving a speech, it will appear rehearsed and artificial… no one likes this because it makes the story boring. If your story comes off as a lecture, your audience may end up becoming defensive and defiant.

The best case scenario here is to sound as if you are having a conversation with the people in front of you. A conversation is a two-way communication. This means that when you speak, you leave pauses in your presentation where audience members are encouraged to participate. This could be giving comments, asking questions, or simply voicing their agreement for what you have to say. Try making the presentation multi-dimensional.

One key thing you shouldn't do is keep a conversation volume. Speak loud and clear and not like you're in a coffee shop with your buddy.

The First Minute:

The first minute of your story is the most powerful part – during this time, you will be making that first impression. You will be determining whether the audience will continue to listen to what you are saying, or whether they will tune you out.

During this time, your voice should be powerful and clear in delivery. During the first minute, you will be creating the "wow" factor. You need to use words that are intriguing and impressive, giving the audience the hunger that is needed for them to listen to your story to the end.

You need to make that first minute count. If there is a moment that people are more receptive, it would be the first 60 to 90 seconds of the speech. The beginning is crucial because during this time, you will be establishing that relationship with your audience.

The problem is some speakers use this time to get comfortable with the stage, while others take the first minute to thank people.

The most effective ways to immediately engage the audience includes stating startling statistics. Shocking the audience with facts and figures that they don't normally hear about will definitely make them want to know more. Opening with a question is also another effective way to grab the audience's attention. Basically a conversation starts with a question and that is just what is happening when a speaker asks the audience a question. By doing so, the speaker is involving the crowd in the process already.

By using a question to start the speech, the speaker is, in a way, telling the audience that "This event is not just about me." Bringing the audience in an enlarged conversation will definitely make them listen.

Your voice is essential to giving a persuasive presentation, as human beings respond in different ways to what they hear. Consider the tone of your voice your non-verbal communication, and also take note that 90% of a message is understood not by the words that are said, but by the accompanying actions and tone that back up these words. Pay attention to other powerful speakers and note the way they use their voices to bring the message forward. You can do this by closing your eyes and just listening. You will be able to pick up when they are emphasizing a point, and when they are pulling people in with their words. Use this knowledge to your advantage.

Chapter Eight: Tips to Dazzle Your Audience

Create a "Wow Story"

What is a good story that wows? Is it only a matter of leading an extraordinary life and having stuff to narrate to others? Yes and no.

It's important that you have a plot that can grip others. Let's just say that many people are quite addicted to their own stories and memories, but few are skilled in actually telling stories.

First of all, you have to detach yourself from your own narratives and see them from the perspective of your audience, no matter what context you find yourself in. Does it captivate other people? It can, especially if your story contains universal truths or objectively sensational incidents. Moreover, a story wows when its style is as powerful as its plot. In other words, you should have a few meaningful and impactful incidents that you can use as the raw material for realistic stories that are nevertheless not ordinary.

Write Down the Story Before Your Presentation:

Personally, I find that it is always effective to write down your story in a few details before you have to speak and use it in public. It will help you narrate it with an emphasis on what is striking and enlightening one way or another for the public – by writing your story down beforehand you already turn into a kind of audience yourself and you can see what grabs attention. Stress those parts and list everything in chronological order. You can start by listing every little incident that was part of the story somehow and you'll prune your narrative later.

It's a form of brainstorming that should help you tap into your memories and your imagination. Don't hesitate to use your creativity to make your story more impactful. However, you should also stick to facts, especially if the story is related to a serious presentation whose purpose is not only pure entertainment.

If you're a comedian, of course you can afford to invent more than others. In order to have a good idea of how your story can impact your public, you should record it or simply narrate it in front of a friend.

Don't Forget About the Power of Emotion:

Emotion is powerful, and I'm sure you know this, so don't forget about emotion while you're telling that story.

You need to realize the importance of both verbal and nonverbal language in order to convey and stir emotions. Use them both in conjunction and synchrony. For example, if you are planning on starting a story about an unexpected incident that happened while you were visiting a different state, you need to hook the public from the start with the emotion that is at the core of your story.

It's as if you prepared your public for all the details to come: Create an emotional vibe in anticipation of what is to come and you will act on people almost subliminally. For example, if during your trip, you met a man on a plane and he told you he was from Berlin during WW2, you're probably going to have a couple of stories to share that aren't going to be on the funny side. You can grab attention by starting your story out with a historical detail that can prepare people emotionally for your own concrete story and experience with the man in question.

During this time, make sure you adjust the tone of your voice accordingly and your audience will sense the emotion that runs through the story they will hear and they'll be curious.

Point blank, when it comes to storytelling, emotion is a very important factor that you cannot leave out. Leaving out emotion in the story will make it dull and boring... you could easily lose people's interest.

Use the Power of Suspense and Variety:

You want to keep your audience hooked, while dazzling them, right? How can you do this? The best way would be to create enough suspense and present things gradually.

Every good story will have a sense of build-up of tension the public can feel themselves. Suspend your story and use anticipative details online. Let that plot unreel according to an organic sense of gradation that replicated real time and chronological order.

Avoid selling your secrets in the beginning. You need to have a recurrent or a highlighted emotion throughout that story ... surprise, amusement, sadness, thrill, and so on. You can do this without using the same scenes all the time. For example, a drama isn't going to repeat the same kind of conflicts between all characters. You need to use variety and lots of sensory details that different from one scene to the next. In addition, you could play with perspective. What I mean here is that if you're presenting one single event, you could switch your perspective from one character to the other in order to underline how different people may have had distinct perceptions or feelings about the same things that happened.

Chapter Nine: Steps of Great Storytelling

For as long as humans have been around, the greatest teachers, entertainers, and leaders have utilized stories when they wanted to communicate a particular message. Storytelling requires you to use various skills in order to engage the audience and draw them into your stories.

In this chapter, we are going to give you the basic steps you can follow in order to take a simple story and transform it into something powerful and worth remembering.

Step One: Develop a Story

If you don't already have a story to tell, or something in mind you would like to expand on, grab a pen and a piece of paper and get your mind unstuck and start brainstorming. On the paper in front of you, write five categories:

- Who
- What
- When
- Where
- Why

The 5 Ws, something I was taught in school which has is probably the only thing I still use from back then…

Next, fill in those blank spaces to one or all of these questions...

- If I was able to do something right now, I would...
- If I had the option to go anywhere tomorrow, I would go to...
- The thing that makes me laugh the most is ...
- When I was (pick an age), I thought a lot about ...
- To me, friends are...
- Today, I learned...

Use these questions to help you create a story (e.g. Who was there?) These are a couple examples of things that will help you get started with creating and telling stories. If you have already developed your own brainstorming style, then of course, you can stick with that ... basically, do whatever works for you.

Step Two: Add Emotion

Honestly, this right here is one of the best ways to tell a story... add emotion. We have found that this is something that is easier for a woman to do than a man. But men, if you want your stories to be unforgettable and impactful, you must add emotion in there. Whether it is the funniest thing you've ever seen or heartbreaking, if you aren't capable of adding any emotion to your story, the listener will have trouble related.

First, start out by closing your eyes and reliving that moment in your life. Actually take time to see yourself doing it or being there again, as if you were out of your body, watching everything take place. Visualize and re-experience it completely in your mind. While you're doing this, you should be able to conjure strong emotions that you can add in storytelling. When you tell the story, relive those emotions as if you're re-experiencing it at that very place and time. When you do this, the listener will be able to hear the emotions in your voice. So, the more you can feel the emotion as you're telling the story, the catchier your story is going to be.

Take note that when you're trying to put some emotion in there, you shouldn't overdo it or make it "overdramatic" because this will cause the listener to become exhausted while trying to listen to you.

Step Three: Enjoy Your Own Story

When you're telling a story to someone, you want them to enjoy the story you're telling, correct? In order to do this, you must first enjoy your own story. Therefore, make sure you choose a story that has a lesson behind it, is interesting, funny, etc.

The key is to have fun with the story and play around with the details – maybe you could try adding a touch of lightheartedness or maybe even sarcasm. See how it makes you feel as you imagine yourself telling the story. If the story provokes the emotional impact you are wanting, then go ahead and keep it as it is, only slightly adjusting it to each listening. If the story doesn't work, toss out the detail you just added and try something different.

The more enjoyable the story is for you, the more entertaining it is going to be for your listener.

Step Four: Don't Forget to Add Pauses

When you're telling a story, you cannot forget those pauses. As a good storyteller, you'll know that a pause can do many things.

As stated in the earlier chapters, pauses are crucial to any speech. It allows everyone to have a breather, takes notes and repeat everything in their heads to make sure they retain it. A pause will also allow you get a reaction to what action/words you just used. Such as a joke, you can take a pause to take in what everyone thought your suggestion to increasing their business.

Whenever creating the story, take your time to carefully time where you would like your pauses. It's always better planning these however sometimes it's better to do these on the fly because you can adapt rather than sticking to your script.

Step Five: Use Body Language

Your body language as explained earlier has a huge factor to your audience because the audience is watching you. It's extremely important that you get this part correct because it shows whether you're taking this seriously or not.

For example, if your body position is in a slacking position back over knees, it shows you're basically just a lazy load of sloths. You can't be slacking forward because it shows that you're not enthusiastic about your own story. Or if you're in a somewhat vulnerable position such as not moving and stationary then you're showing that you're not confident about what you're saying. These things are what people look out for and if you're faking it, people will see right through you.

Make sure you add gestures such as showing how big something is or how miniscule they are. Then just start waving your arms randomly every now and then. It may sound stupid but everyone does it and creates some sort of engagement towards the audience.

You need to master body language by practicing in front of the mirror (this is a classic technique). Nowadays, people may also use their smart phone to record themselves and watch the video.

Mastering body language is very hard for introverts because we have to force it out but for extroverts, it should be easier. One way of making sure you've got everything is right just performing infront of your friends or a camera then re-watching it or asking for opinions.

Step Six: Have a Point to Your Story

Don't be blabbing around. I've seen too many people blabbing around like how they met their wife in some business seminar. It's simply not needed. Cool, some context is nice but there's no point in having it as half of your presentation. Just get straight to the point then expand your points within your story if you need it to be longer.

Your story has to have a base to it such as how to grow the audience's business. Get straight to that point as telling why it's useful then they'll take the talk more seriously then you can get to the real meat such as telling them how to advertise etc.

Chapter Ten: The Psychology Behind Storytelling

Storytelling is something that is rooted deep in our psychology, which in turn is mostly a result of our evolutionary development as a species. Human beings value patterns – we notice and value cause and effect. It's what allows us to make sense of the world around us.

At its core, a story is just that: a train of cause and effect. The teller recounts an event that led to another, which in turn led to another, and so on until they reach a conclusion. This is generally how the real world works, and we gained our massive advantage over other species when we learned to recognize this.

It's for this reason that narrative, the way that things come together in a logical sequence is so important to us. We see it in the world around us, and we massively enjoy discovering it. Stories engage that deep-seated desire for narrative, satisfying it by giving the listener a glimpse into how it works in the life of the person telling the story.

If you have a message, there are two ways you can go about delivering it. Suppose you want to share with an audience of young people who want to pursue the same career you have. You could just give them a sterile list of everything they have to do to achieve what you have – the areas of study they will have to specialize in, the amount of work they will have to put in, the obstacles they will face – in a general sense that isn't too tailored to any individual. You'd use wording like "most successful actors had to live for years taking low-paying bit parts as extras. I

In commercials" or "if you want to be a successful realtor, you will have to intimately understand how the housing market works". On the other hand, you could give your advice in the form of a story – in this case your story in particular. An actor could tell the story of his own period of lowly paid obscurity, and the realtor could give personal anecdotes of what she studied, how much time and effort it took you and the obstacles she faced. If some aspects of the climb to where they are now did not apply to them, they could fill those gaps in with the stories of your colleagues.

On the surface the first approach seems like it would work very well – the advice would apply to everyone, leaving no space for anyone to think it wouldn't work for them in particular. But in reality the second approach would in fact be far more effective. Studies have shown that after a certain period, only 5-10% of information that is passed on as simple data remains fresh and vivid in the mind of the person receiving it, but an astonishing 65-70% of information passed on in the form of stories is retained. Why is this so?

Well, the reason for this is that simple data activates areas of the brain that decipher meaning... and nothing else. Raw data just isn't very stimulating at all. When listening to a story, however, some very interesting things happen in the brain. Parts of the brain that would be activated if the person listening were actually doing the things being described are activated. If the storyteller is describing a movement, say like walking or dancing, the motor cortex, which is responsible for controlling our movement's lights up. If the storyteller describes a sensory input, like a smell, a taste or the feeling of a texture, the sensory cortex, which decodes actual sensory inputs is activated. This is on top of the reactive emotions we experience when listening to a story: a description of a tense or frightening situation induces anxiety and fear by proxy, and the resolution of such situations brings palpable relief. Descriptions of love and happy situations give us that warm, fuzzy feeling inside as if we are experiencing them ourselves.

As a result, a story far more easily and permanently imprints itself in the memories of the listener. The details of the story and the emotions it brings up in this way act as a delivery mechanism for your information or message, carrying it along and helping it 'stick' in the audience's brains. One particular demonstration of the power of stories to imprint themselves in the brain of a listener is how they sometimes become such a big part of their psyche that they begin to tell the story as if they were present or as if it actually happened to them. Sure, a lot of times this is done for simple effect, or as outright theft, but an astonishing number of times it's actually completely unconscious. The story was so well told, the images it left so vivid that the listener has completely forgotten that it didn't actually happen to them.

The value of a story isn't just dependent on the type of information it gives to the audience. The emotions and reactions it creates can be immensely valuable just by themselves. Implanting emotions in the brain of another person the way a story does is a hugely powerful thing, helping their brains to come in sync with yours. This can be of great value when you are trying to convince others to think your way – priming them with your own patterns of thought and feeling makes them much more open to any other ideas you may wish for them to adopt. Telling the story of an event or circumstance that shaped who you are can affect your audience the very same way as the event itself affected you.

On the whole, we can deduce that there are four main objectives one wishes to achieve when telling a story. In no particular order, they are – to entertain, to inform, to instruct and to inspire. All stories aim to achieve some combination of these, and they are usually the most efficient and long-lasting way of doing it. This is the power, the lightning that this book aims to help you cage and harness to your benefit – the ability to influence the minds of others and leave your imprint on the world through sharing your stories.

Conclusion

Let me ask you a question – right now, how is your confidence level? Surely, it has elevated since you have read this book and you are ready to approach your next storytelling event with confidence. This is because you have read a book full of secrets and by going through these secrets, you now feel as if you are able to face any situation during your storytelling presentation.

You are now clear about the way that storytelling events have changed over time, moving from the traditional methods that were static and featured considerable written information, to the modern methods that are more fluid, incorporating pictures and other visual aids to bring the method forward.

By now, you probably understand why the best presenters get excited about their presentation. Excitement affectis passion, helps one to become more prepared and ensures that you are armed with the tools needed for a successful event.

Telling a story involves more than the words that you speak, it also involves the way that you say those words, and how your body confirms what you have to say is important and supported by facts and information. This is what makes it possible for you to connect with the audience, and to create an impression that lasts and carries you forward.

With these useful techniques and secrets at your disposal, you will never be caught off guard, and you will be capable of delivering an exceptional story to your audience, each time. Your audience will be able to relate to you, and you will appear as if you're an expert.

Please if you enjoyed this book, I would greatly appreciate it if you gave an honest review of it. Those honest words would be more than just words to me but feedback for my next book!

Also, please check out my other books!

Thanks for reading my book.

www.ingramcontent.com/pod-product-compliance
Lightning Source LLC
Chambersburg PA
CBHW070334190526
45169CB00005B/1889